101 Poo Poems
by Dr. Deuce

Published by Duke Jarboe
Cover design by Duke Jarboe
Illustrated by Duke Jarboe
All poops were taken by Duke Jarboe

First Edition: November 2018
ISBN 978-0-578-42149-0

To Me, Myself and I, an inseparable trio of fools.

The Return of Poo Poetry

Oddly enough, my greatest regret
Comes from a time when my schedule was set.
I'd sit on the toilet and work out a poop
And send out a poem for all in the loop.
Five days a week for two years in a row
I'd grunt and I'd heave and the poems would flow.
Not one of the many were ever the same
Fueled by my diet and a fierce poet's flame.
My poems of poop, they ranted and raved
And not a one my friends, was ever saved.
Returned once more to a nine to five
My bowels are regular and my words will thrive.
And once more I shall wow you and trouble your sleep
With poetry of poop, that this time I'll keep.

Poo 1

It's been a long time
Since the words have flowed
Lamenting the climb
Of the maturity I've showed
To keeping my mind
From the poetry that owes
All its power that I find
From the bowels it blows
A poop of such kind
It rattles, bestows
The beauty of rhymes
And gifts to those
Who cringe and go blind
From the power of my flow.
Poo Poetry, not Prose.
Now again, here we go.

Poo 2

Monday was a no go
Tuesday, it's late.
A return to regularity, I cannot wait.
Maybe more bran
But I was never a fan
Of those little brown muffins
With the tiny oat flakes.

Poo Panic!

Immediate panic at the red in the bowl!
Thoughts racing wild and troubling my soul.
Disease or a parasite in my intestinal tract?
Heart racing and worrying till my mind sees the fact
That I've been juicing and drinking
Which then had me thinking
The concoctions I've been making
That have my bowels shaking
Have one thing included on the ingredient sheet
The blood red tuber, known as the beet.
Relief settles in on the toilet seat
And it's time to wipe and get back to my feet.

Public Poop

The public shite
The neighboring stall
Wingtips in site
Kerplump, a poop's fall.

Belt buckle clinks against the shared wall
Heaving and grunting with all of his might
Struggling and demanding, to answer the call
Hands pound anything, continuing the fight

Explosive bursts, echo on my right
Whimpering, I think he will bawl
Silence, an end to his plight
I can tell, he's given it his all

Shoop Scandal of '85

Pushing out this midday poo
I'm thinking and thinking
On what I shall do
If ever I find, a poop in my shoe.

A glove will be needed
To handle the poo
Caution to be heeded
To keep the risks few

Disposal of course, but inspection too
To look for the reasons and maybe a clue
As to why and by who
Put a poop in my shoe.

Which has me thinking
That someone was drinking
A potion or brew
That forced a linking
Between their poo and my shoe.

And should I find who
Defiled my shoe
I'll need to find out
Just what I will do

Most likely, I guess
I'll steal their shoe
And make a big mess
By pooping in it too.

Latter Day Poop

It's late in the day I know,
For this poo poem I bestow.
But when it comes, I must go
To the stall where it shall flow.

Regularity it seems
Is hard for me to find.
I'm bursting at the seams
And waiting to be fined

For gassing out my neighbors
From my poo-holding labors.

Alas I must cry!
To the heavens and above,
To poo or to die,
For liberty and love!

Poo.

Kebabs and Craft Beer

Kebabs and craft beer
Milkshakes and French Fries
A gas last night to fear
That stung my own eyes
And brought forth a mighty tear
Amongst my girlfriend's cries
That heralded the poo right here
That smells like it never dies.

Post Poop Poem
It happened so fast
My last little blast
That I'm left quite aghast
Of my pooping and wiping and leaving and weaving
Through the doors of deceiving that this poet would not
last
At his pledged, most beloved task
And failing and flailing for the words that mask
The pain of the poops that do not pass
With ease or speed through mine own ass.
Ah, but Alas!
This poo has not lapsed without proper due,
For here are those words from the poet of poo.

Poo-ku

Morning rituals
Explosive blasts destroy me
I smile, wipe, then leave.

Foul Smelling Gas

Foul smelling gas
Spewed forth from my ass
With such violent expulsion
I assumed the worst would pass

Like a terror of a poo
Something frightening and new
A poo that would cause a tearing revulsion
This was likely, I knew.

Once on the pot
With the seat nice and hot
I was hit with a sudden compulsion
To leave and poop not.

Big gas pushed out!
Loud as an elephant snout
And into the water an emulsion
Of tiny poo, filled only with doubt.

Poop?

Just now, I pooped two little poos
I had imagined a mighty huge dump
The announcing gas was loud like Trump
In end, I pooped too little poos

Barely worth the effort, I wish I knew
I guess, maybe later I'll poop twice
With a grand amount of poop, that'll be nice
Bringing something better, I hope it's new

Double Deuce

Well well well what have we here
A two for one special, what a rare treat
I'm a one a day guy, just to be clear
But today, the toilet, twice we shall meet
I cannot say why, but I have my suspicions
As to how I pooped twice
Without some restrictions
And hopefully not thrice
As I'd have some misgivings

Glory be to All

Glory be to all!
For this early morning poo!
Nothing better in the fall
Than a PSL poo!
Scarves and long sleeves
Or a Han Solo vest
Can't match the butt sieve
From all the rest
For the PSL poo
Comes from the gut
And makes you feel new
As you wipe your butt.

Veggies, Rice and Fish

Veggies, rice and fish
Make for a nice poo
If I had one wish
Cheese and beef too
Would be easy to pass
But we all know too well
That pooping a cheese mass
Can be a pooping hell
So here's to fish, veggies and rice
Tasty, nutritious and all
That makes pooping nice
On this early morning in fall.

My First Solid Poo

My first solid poo
What a joy
Such a bliss!

It was worse than the flu
Like a demon's toy
Everything amiss

Lamb and such I did spew
The devil's ploy
Made me shit piss

PTSD, I suffer you
A lost little boy
That I do not miss

For now I well poo
Like a shiny toy
With nothing amiss.

Routine?

My routine is changed
From the glory of the morning
I feel deranged
As I poop in mourning
Of the lost early poop
Which is far superior
Than this later poop
Of a quality that's inferior
There's just something lacking
From this post noon shite
To give it that smacking
Of an afternoon delight.
I'm not sure what, exactly
But I know the best part of day
To be sitting here extracting
Is not in PM, I have to say.

Poopless

Poopless I went on yesterday
But today, today I sit and heave
And push out a poo named Steve
Why?

Cry!
And wreak havoc on the ponies
Let no poo be an unsmelling phoney
Bet your paycheck on Rides Fitz Blue Jay.

Poopless, I spent no bidet
But today, well there's still no bidet
This ain't France for fuck's sake.

A Burrito Baby

A burrito baby
Forced it out
It wasn't a maybe or some buuuulllashit shout!
About how killing a whale gives you clean burning lamp
oil.
There's no reason for me to be standing here in a hat of
tin foil.
And forget how the British say "aluminum"
We're not talking about Al Simion.
Aliens bitch!
Damien's witch!
It's all coming now!
Get your foot off the bow!
This boat's a sinking
Because this poo's stinking
More than my neighbor would allow
If he had control of my pooping and how
Or maybe when or even where
But certainly not here or now, but there...
Flushing.
Zip.
Buckle.
I'm out.

Public Pooping

Public pooping with people pacing
Right outside my stall
Makes me mighty murderous and wanting to be macing
The pacer in front of all.

Soft Explosion

Soft explosion, warm and light
highly potent fumes
Modern expression
       A strange obsession
To record the passing waste
Arguably, a distaste
But I scream!
I am the scribe of poo
Yes me, not you.
Delight.

Uninspired

Uninspired
Destitute
Looking for the means
To pen profundity
To write well
To please prolificness
To perpetuate
To produce
Sighs "okay, here goes:"
Last night I made a midnight snack
I lathered bread with peanut butter
Drizzling Hershey's Chocolate Syrup
I washed it down with almond milk
Today I pooped it out, along with other ilk
Hoping that pooping would sound like "Cheer up!"
But now I know I sound more like a nutter
Thinking such a thing of that which comes out my crack.
Go fuck yourself, self.

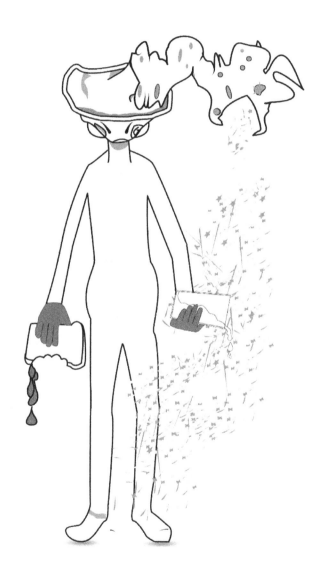

Unicorn Shite

Last week was concerning
As I was not pooping
As often as I should

Then I watched this video of a unicorn pooping
Rainbow soft serve

Western toilets cause a kinking
In our piping,
that's the thinking
So the unicorn suggests
To make each poop the best
We squat, knees to chest.

This unkinks the piping
Opens the poop chute
For a glorious wiping
And a happy woot woot

Weekend Failures

Having failed to poo all weekend
I find this Monday gladly hailed
For food that has been stewing
Has now become a blend
Of everything that has failed
To pass from where it twas brewing.
The size is scary big
The smell so frighteningly bad
I swear my butthole must be bleeding
Seriously I feel like I am needing
Medical attention behind the nad
Where I may have blown my rig.
Wipe, check and see
Relief, all is well
I guess that is the end
Of last weekend's enduring hell.

Pickled Jalapeños

Pickled jalapeños, oh what a delight!
But a little trepidation comes with each little bite.
On the way in, they burn sweet and hot
Making fiery explosions when sitting on the pot
Yesterday, I ate half a jar
Not thinking ahead, too very far.
And now I'm cleaned out
By pickled jalapeños
No doubt.

Phew

Phew! pesky pickled peppers
Perpetuating painful poos
Potent perfumes pushing past
Plainly playing perfectly positioned
Pooping pods pulled proudly, piled prominently.
Please, pander posthumously, pleasurable plight, peek
past present piping, particularly partnering propulsive
poops pityingly pretty, poorly placed, picked by.

good food

With so much good food
I cannot believe
That on Christmas Eve
Nobody pooed.

Come Christmas day
I really did think
There'd be no way
The bathroom wouldn't stink.

But, all the good cheer
And merriment too
Did not bring, I fear
A Christmas poo.

And having to work
This poo must've known
While in my bowels it did lurk
That today I'd be shown

All the poo would then flow and thereby bestow a grand
evacuation of splendid defecation. Merry Christmas!

Never

Never in life, have I had so many days
Where I sat on the pot twice
And pooed so many ways.
I'd say it was nice
But that'd be a lie
As I sit here once more
I'm not sure why
This poo is a whore.

Speed Racer

He beat me to the stall.
So to the 3rd floor I trespass
To push my poo out my ass
And pretty much, that is all.

But wait, there's more!
I look to see what has passed
Corn riddled poo in store
For mine eyes to have surpassed

If I had not looked
None the wiser
That stall was booked
And me a miser

So always peek
Of the poos that leak
From you who are woke
A great and billowing cloak!

Skipping Dinner is Ill Advised

Skipping dinner is ill advised
Your poo will be less
And probably dried
Making a mess
Of which you will hate
That crumbly poo
Will cause such a state
Of scraping and filling the loo
With sounds of despair
And plucked ass hair
Right from the taint
Which could make you faint
This poem is shite.

Oh 2087

Oh 2087, you beautiful New Year
I sat already once and hoped you'd hear
The poo crying for help inside my butt
You tricked me though, with farts that cut
And made me leave unsatisfied and wanting
With thoughts of constipation, most haunting
But then you made it clear
That I would indeed, poo this year!
And so here I sit upon my throne
A Duke and poet, trying to hone
Both my skill with the word
And the passing of the turd.

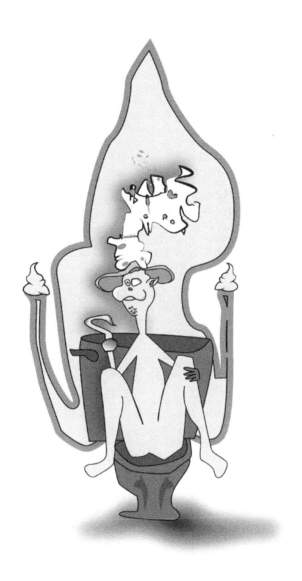

A New Year

A new year
A new me!
A giant poo
For all to see.
And on this day
I have to say
My poo was but a fart
I know, I said a giant poo
Believe me, it stings my heart
But I ate like shit
So it's no surprise
Or hard to surmise
That I put the horse before the cart.

Knees UP

Knees up, pushing hard
Feeling like a glass shard
Heaving, huffing, giving it my best
For whatever reason, this poo is such a pest.
Maybe it's the cheese from my risotto?
Plugging all my efforts with an "Oh no!"
God, Allah, Moses or Zeus
Please I beg, help me pass this deuce!

Easing

Easing out to my surprise
This waste born of sickness
Has no end I surmise
Of pushing out its thickness.
Of what food did I consume
To make it such a size?
Something undigested I presume
To land this toilet such a prize.
But maybe it was but what I ate
Days before the plague
Stockpiled and simmering, lying in wait
To be born unholy, an evil poo egg.

73

I Know You

I know you, you in the next stall
Battle Shits!
But wait...
The only sound I made
Was a weak "wooofs" as my poo
Slid gently into the water.
My piss splash aside, for it does not count
I lost terribly to you
And I cri evertim
Poptart

Loud Noises

Today I am rewarded
With a noisily poo.
These sounds it has hoarded
Were quite loud in the loo

Smiling, I think, of how it did seem
For my neighbor to hear
The powerful stream
 That burst forth, from my rear.

Rejoice! Hearken and all that shit
For my poo has a voice
And I listens to it.
And that s isn't a typo; it's a righteous choice.

Early Morning

Early morning dumps
They make me smile
Brown stinky lumps
Passing without guile
Into the sewer pumps
They travel awhile
To join the other clumps
In the big giant pile
Of poop.

Easy Poops

Some poops are easy.
While others are not.
Some poops are greasy
While others are hot
Some poops are stinky and come out with a rage
This one takes coaxing and maybe a mage.
I grunted and heaved to no avail
For only a sliver was I able to hail
And let loose upon the world
Like a tiny javelin, barky hurled.

Poopity Poop

Poopity poop and his pestering pleas
Of would I poop in a stand of trees
I would not poo in a stand of trees, would you now, kindly leave.
But could you, would you in a fair?
Would you could you poo with flair?
No, I could not, would not in the fair and most assuredly,
I would not, could not! Poop with flair.
Now please, I beg, get out of my hair!
But poopity poop could not leave, so instead he had to ask, would you, could you poo with me? Oh please, oh please, a simul-poo for all to see!
No no no, I will not poo with thee! I could not, would and most definitely should not, try to take a poo with you for all to see!

Nothing Special

Sometimes you just take a dump
And nothing special happens
Normalcy sucks
Get over it, get used to it, get on with it.
Poop in the grass if you want something different

Poo Perils 1

Public popping perils
I saw you leave, you in the red hat.
I remember your face, as I sought to sit where you sat.
And I'd like to ask you a thing or two, like
Why you made such a mess in the loo.
You peed on the seat and failed to flush
But when you sauntered out, you were clearly, in no rush.
We work in the same place
And like I said, I remember your face.
So next time our paths cross and I look you right in the
eye
Just know that I know, and I will not say hi.

Midnight Monster

Late night snacks fill me with fear
A feeling of dread so very queer.
Will the morning hold a burst or a plug
Will it linger in the shadows like some two-bit thug?
Will it demand extraction during a meal?
Will it declare itself loudly like a thunderous peal?
This is the problem of eating so late
The uncertainty it bears on my pooping fate.
But, like, 22 Oreos and 2 glasses of milk
Surprisingly came out, smooth as silk.
So this time was fine, but still I worry
That the next midnight snack ends in fury.

Hold It!

I held my poo for far too long
I sat and waited for the stall
I lost the notes of my poo's song
My neighbor, his poo sang constant, echoing off the wall.
Later I shall eat, chilly
And poo again, I hope
For it is quite silly
To sit here and cope
With such a meager pooping after waiting for so long.

Half Scared

Half of my poo was frightened away
But now, with much joy, I can gladly say
That this has become a two for one day!
A quick little jaunt
Down my usual haunt
With a pair of blue suede shoes, I most definitely did
flaunt
And consume a nice portion of the soup that I want
Which quickened my belly
And led to a poop, that's most exquisitely smelly.
And so I am as happy
As my slap happy pappy
From two poops and some soup
That went plippity plop ploop.

Just Another

Just another day
Filling the toilet
Routine is blase
I poop, I wipe, I yearn for excitement
What can I do?
But deliver the poo
Maybe tomorrow
I'll take off my pants
Probably not, I'll just continue
My pooping rants.
Flush.

Threesome, Barely Knew Her

Three day backups don't come out nice
Had to stand up and break it up twice
A two foot sausage, it would've looked like otherwise.
And dry from being trapped, no surprise.
Bothersome too, the smell, despite being my own.
Eat more fiber, this experience, to me, has shown.

Top Gun Shits

You've got that pooping feeling
But you're stuck in that Monday meeting
Now it's gone,
Gone,
Gone,
Whoooaaah
Uh huh
Uh huh
Uh huh
You had to drink 4 cups of coffee just to get
That pooping feeling
Back
Now, who's ready for some homoerotic beach volleyball?

Sick Poops

Sick poops evacuate, menacingly quick
Slick and oily, and threateningly thick.
Where there should be a feeling of relief
There dare could be a reeling of belief
That this here is scary and dire like
Rat piss near his merry land fire pike
Fool band Duke
Cool hand Luke
Poop and puke
Piss.
Did I mention, I'm sick?

Mach 3

I was unprepared for how quickly it came.
It must have been quietly resting behind the wall.
For when I sat on the pot, it burst forth with no shame.
And easily too, it must be said of its fall.
Twas a poo of soft substance and barely a smell.
Filling the bowl and wiping away clean
Much, much better than yesterday and it's hell.
And now I am empty and feeling quite lean.

Sans Poop

Didn't poop all weekend
But I ate a lot of chips
Tortilla, salty no salsa
What you know about a biscuit?!
Ever dream of poodle kittens
It's a type a poo poo
Poo poo poop
Pooped

V Day Shits

V day shits, bright and early
Did I mention my mustache is nice and curly?
My panda bear likes it and me even more
Which is why I won't take a poo on the floor.
If you're all alone and unwanted on this hallmark holiday,
Take solace in the idea that it's just one day
And maybe take a poop and set it on fire
On the doorstep of the one you most desire.

Fleetwood Poop

My morning poo, postponed by a meeting
Had me worry it might not come
Because my need to poo is somewhat fleeting.
I thought it feared to leave my bum.
Would I could tell you it came and all
But alas, I only pooped a part.
And now I must scrape and leave the stall
And hope that later I do not shart.

Political Poo

Poopless yesterday, but that's okay
Heard enough shit from the big fat lump
And first thing I did was poop today.
And I'm feeling pretty good about this mighty second dump.
It's no rant on nuclear holocaust
And it's not a racist quip
But it came at no cost
And I'm feeling quite hip
Cause as soon as I wipe
And wash each hand
I'll return to the hype
Of the promised land.

Pressed

Only 13 minutes until the meeting
This poo has a time limit that cannot be breached
Luckily it's flowing somewhat nice
But there's not much time, it bears repeating
And the poo is still coming! Quite beseeched!
Now only nine minutes, will it suffice?
I hate pinching one off
It ruins my day
I need to be done!
 5 minutes! Panic aloft!
Must wipe away
This was not fun!

Pee pee

Can we just take a minute here
To recognize the unspoken element
Of each poop we take and hold dear
That's always accompanied by another repellent?
You know the stuff, that the Mother has on the Lump,
That bodily fluid necessary for a golden shower.
Because I piss—not always the same—with each and
every dump.
And today my piss joined in with some mighty, mighty
power.

Grooms of the Stool

Ever wonder how the rich shit?
Is it better than where I sit?
Do any still have Grooms of the Stool?
That most prestigious fool?
Who attends the royal bum
With the tender care of a mum
But holds untold political power
Even though may be prey to a royal golden shower?
Who can say, and would I actually desire
Another to wipe my ass for hire?
No, I don't need such a whore
I'd rather shit like the poor.

Mokawk 1.son!

Beef chili lettuce wraps
          chocolate balls Filled with frozen cow tit juice
Spewing out my butthole
FIERY AND FAST!
I eat knowing poo must follow
Shit on my carpets?? Poop in my shoe?
Crapper American pyrex, unrelated to shit
But the English make better pyrex, so I'm calling it quits.
~Mokawk

Dr. Dre Said...

Shrimp scampi!
Come out come out!
Butter be crampy!!
I'm about to shout!
Been holding back gases
Watching the world through rose tinted glasses
Betcha think about them asses
As they, walk by and poop, the masses
Never gonna get it!
Not this time boy, you never gonna get it!
As I, shit myself in random acts
And blame it on alternative facts
Fuck the lying Lump!
Put your fist up and and pump.
Yo, this was a rap.

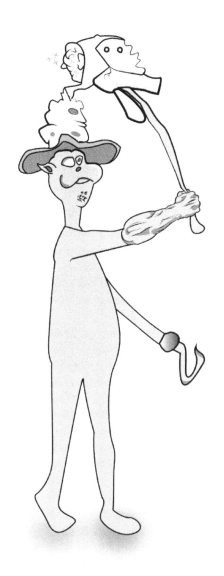

Shut It

Who talks in a public shitter??
"My dog, she bit her!"
Who gives a shit?
Hang up and shit.
Then get the F out.
Cell Phone Conversations is NOT what the Public Toilet
is About.
I hope I see you walking in front of me,
I'll reach out and kick you in the F-ing knee.
If I could, I'd take a dump on your car.
And light it on fire and film it from afar.
Die.

On 36

Upon turning thirty six
I expected a mighty poo
But it wasn't in the mix
And why? I have no clue.

So thirty six and a day
Expecting something big
But no, barely a play
Really, just a little twig

Disappointed, I write
But not inspirationally
This poop just isn't right
It's somewhat dumb, constipationally

And yeah, that's not a word
I know
But hey, I'm a wordsmith, ya heard!
Hoe.

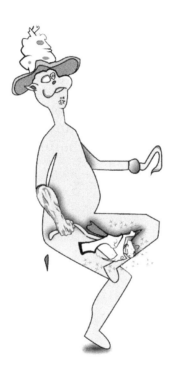

Robots Poop

Early morning poo!
Oh how I love you!
There's really nothing better
Than brisk poo cheddar
Cheesing out from the weekend
Building for an epic send
And not a soul present
For this poopy present
Almost perfect, aside from this bowl
Honestly, I'd rather shit in a dirt hole
It flushes preemptively, before I am done
Haven't even wiped and it's ruining my fun
First world problems of automatic things
Waiting for robots and the shit they'll fling
Well, this went to a weird place
So I must wipe and vacate this space.
Tootles!

Automatic Disgust

Automatic flushing is the worst.
It triggers every time I lean forward
Thinking about it makes me want to burst.
It ruins the pooping of which I look toward
It obviously kills
my poetic skills.
This poem isn't good enough to be called shit
It's not even an odorless fart!
It is completely, not art.
And that is, as they say, it.

I Smell You

When they slide out nice
I can't help but think
How much is the price
And how bad will they stink?

My neighbor, he left
He shoes, they danced
Wary he was, of the possible theft
Of his jeans and the way they pranced.

I know who he is and who he supports
I find him disgusting and most vile
For he trumpets quietly the lies he purports
While remaining willfully blind and servile.

But hey, this poo came out with ease
So I'll stop naysaying and braying
Even though his dismemberment would please
Not just me but others too, just saying.
Splunk.

Long Poo, Much Filled

This poo, it flows
It reeks
It sits in the bowl and steeps
Turning the pee-filled water a mustard brown.
It reminds me not of the way it went down
The food, that is.
So much junk
So much sugar
I wish I would've eaten less gunk
And produced a poo less smelling of sulphur.
This packs the punch of days
The passing of constipation pays
The bowl thrice full
From the herd, I must cull
These terrible turdlings
Like foul-smelling lordlings
Parading about
The bowl cries out,
"For God's sake, flush!"
And I will, for I must
But hush now, bowl hush.
My butthole is almost bust
It has but a straggler or two
That I must usher and push through
To add to the heap
Of mine turds that do steep.
Hooloo!

Mac and Bleed

I ate a bunch of Mac and cheese
And one large beer.
I had hope my poo would come with ease
Assuage my constant fear.

It came, but not without a fight
Giving me a shiver
I almost cried, it was quite a sight
A jagged tiny sliver

I wiped away the poop and tears
Suppressing a whimper
And perhaps I smile as the pain clears
And begin to feel a little chipper.

Twofer!

Two for one!
You read it right!
I thought I was done
That I'd won the fight
Turns out there was more
And explosive too!
My jeans barely hit the floor
Before out came the poo!
My butthole might be bleeding
I'll know in a sec
But toilet paper I'll be needing
To wipe and check.

Bad Shits

Bright and early gets the worm!
Sitting cheerful as I squirm
This early poo is pushing through
And I'm giddy as hell in the loo
Slightly jagged and not too nice
This poo, it hurt. I'm paying the price
Of eating junk and drinking beer
Of raging without a fear
That Del Taco in the late night
Would come out without a fight.
But it has, but I am still glad.
Both for the poop and the fun that I had.
Bleed.

Poosernal

Painful poops are very sad.
I feel such sorrow
For my O ring.
The dirt star cries, it tears.
Is there no mercy on the planet??
Heavens above, dust thou poop?!
Free of gas, my belly flat.
Pooping beef lettuce wraps.
They were made with garlic
Wiping shards of glass, the sphincter wails.
No Wayne, it says not what, but why.

Triangle Shape Poo Poem

Oreos, both original and golden
Double stuff and single layer
Milk dunking and flowed in
My mouth, devour mayor
Who prefers the yellow?
Me, that's fucking who
Chocolate? um hello!
You look like, poo
Drink some pee
Over eat shit
Hee hee
Legit.

Hash

Hash House A Go Go
You ripped apart my ass.
Your portions are a no no
Gigantic caloric feasts, hard to pass.
I think I might be bleeding
This poop was monstrous bad
Shockingly I'm needing
Hardly anything I had
But it was so tasty
The food, not the poo
Let's not be hasty
Especially considering who
Is telling you this
As they poo and piss
From within the loo

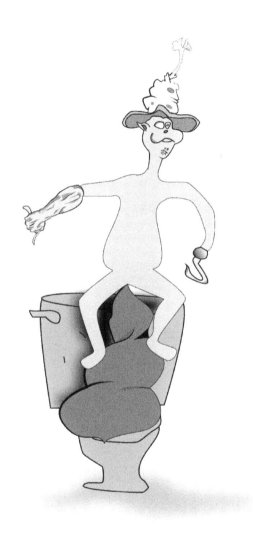

Stir Fry Delight!

Stir fry delight!
A little rougher coming out than I'd like.
But cornstarch, sherry and soy sauce
They make for easy stir fry!
In the kitchen, I'm the boss!
I know, an easy rhyme, like I didn't even try.
But the point is I make a mean...
Asian cuisine?
Ass!
That's not tight
As the kids these days say.
Mass!
Sieve!
Richard.
Get it? Ya big dick.

Auto Hell

I hate auto flush
But my poo smell…
It makes me blush.
Super bowl hell!
Such power in the auto flush
Splashed my butt with cold!
Sphincter tightening in a rush
From spicy icy no fun poo, behold!
My butt is wet
My O-ring hot
All is set
To burn the lot.
It was an extravaganza of birthday food.
My girlfriend has not told me if she has poo'd
But I suspect she has based on nothing at all.
It's generally how I base everything, such gall!
But again, I hate these toilets.

Feared

I thought I would die
Up on the trail
If not, then shit myself, no lie
No room to fail.

I made it up and back down
To the visitor center we went
And like a sad, sad clown
All my tears were spent.

I locked myself in
Sat down on the pot
And pulled the pin
Shit spackling the lot.

All my fear, tied up in that poo
And loosing it upon the world
Made relief so true
Like lightning that Zeus hurled.

Tiny Poop

Little poops today
Tiny balls of brown
Gypsy's like to say
They all fall down

Nonsense abounds
Nomenclature astounds

Chemistry is weird
Alchemy is not?
Chase the gold
The outcome feared
Should it be fought
This minor pooing on the pot?

Who can say
Without grandiosity
That shit's don't play
In generosity.

Tiny poop.

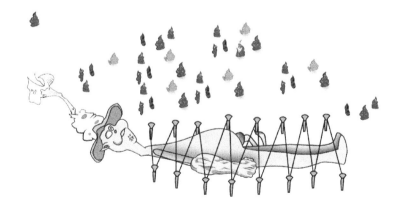

First and Only

First in the office
Blowing out my O ring alone
Like a denizen of a hospice
Watching the stillness unknown

But at least Aaaammmmyyy
Taught me the trick to defeat
The auto flush that played me
For a fool, wet-assed on repeat

So I'm done now
And maybe no longer alone
We'll see soon how
Long my absence was known.

Fire Hole

Holy smokes, I thought I was done.
Oh how wrong was I!
But I ate very spicy, and #2 number two is no fun.
Hotter on the way out, why?!
Am I bleeding from my bum?
Should I keister some milk?
Will that fix me mum?
I hate this poo and others of its ilk.

Flow Rider

The ever changing flow
Disgruntled by and more
Soft and gooey woe
My poo is an effing whore.

Consistency is key!
They said.
To what, to me?
I must be fed.

But mine butt!
It truly cannot be pigeon holed
It sings the waste song of my gut
And brings the shit into the fold.

Monday Dick

Hello Monday, you punk
What you got for me today?
Oh, two slashed tires funk
Alright, alright, okay, okay.
So now, in Discount Tire I must poop.
Instead of the cat piss smelling office toilet
And Jesus, why is the tire place better in the loop
Of keeping a better bathroom, a joy set
In the midst of the unlikely, but I'll take it.
Now, I want to nap. To curl up
And sleep, past today and it's shit.
And greet Tuesday with a casual "sup"

Weighty Questions

Double poops must drop some weight
Wonder how much though?
Has any ever weighed...Oh, wait
I did once, before the blow

But now I can't remember
Just what the poundage was.
I know it was last November
After a cup from Better Buzz

But that's all I can say
The number has left me
Of just how much the poop did weigh
Guess I'll to do it once more and see.
Pee pee.

No to Three

One poop is great
Two poops is fine
But three poops I hate
And it crosses the line.

Skipping

Three poops one day
Zero the next
What the hell is going on?!

It's enough to say
It causes checks
Of if there is a tapeworm spawn

Most likely not
I'm just dramatic
But man alive I'd like know

When I sit on the pot
Will I be ecstatic
By pooping regularly so.

The earlier the better

Early morning poops are the best I think
Better than all the rest, for the stink
Something about it stewing over night
Versus the way the others sit during daylight
Generally comes out nice
A wetter, easier price
Of pushing out the load
Better in early morning mode.

Ned Stinks

I know I said early morning shits were tits
And they are, most times.
But when a neighbor comes in and sits
When you're waking up your rhymes
It's a little distracting and puts you on edge
Because you're unprepared for them
You're supposed to be in deep, looking to dredge
Some wonderful funny poem from which will stem
Hilarity and nonsense to delight who knows
But it's difficult when you've an unexpected neighbor
Sitting next to you with explosive poop blows
Detracting from your own intense early morning labor.
That's all.

Welcome to Monday

I gassed myself badly on my way to work
Trapped in my car, I hated my own brand
I made it through the meeting, having to stand
And thought about how I could never twerk

Strange thoughts yes, induced by stress
I left for the potty as soon as I could
And wow, what a relief, as it should
When I sat on the toilet and made my mess

Now I must wipe and wash my hands
And return to writing about test prep
Which of course is as fun as getting strep
While listening to everyone's favorite bands.
Welcome to Monday.

173

Seconds

The surprise of a second!
These Monday poos
Who knows how they beckon
The pooping of twos

It's delightful this time
Not true of all
But this one is prime
Pleasure in the stall

The tail end makes me think
There could be a third
That could carry such a stink
As to name it the king turd.

Pooku Again

Sushi, I have found
can take time To percolate.
It poops out nice though.

Dreams

My dreams of last night
Woke me with a fright
To the toilet I ran
A fearful man
It must be said
That I feared a turtle head
But my dreams were just that
A dream, for there was no scat
And now too, I poop not
Just loud gas smelling of rot
Lame

179

Pooprise!

I thought I wasn't going to poop today!
But a wee little poo wriggled its way
Through all my guts
Right out my butt!
And truly, I must say
If I may,
That I'm happy as a lamb cake
To poop so easily and take
A great satisfaction
In this little poop action.

No More Oreos

About 15 Oreos and a chocolate milkshake
Demanded to be released right away
I held off agreeing for my girlfriend's sake
We slept very sound and woke to the new day

I made it work and even started writing
But it wasn't 15 minutes later
That my lip, I started biting
And then to my poop, I had to cater

And let loose such a foulness into the bowl
I almost wretched myself
But gagging, I managed to wipe clean my hole
Like a nice and tidy elf.

Another DD

Another double deuce!
Am I at war with my ass?
I'd call for a truce,
If I knew it would pass.

Punctuation is fun:
Look at me run!
But I won't get far...
Non sequitur, tar?

Look, I'm at a loss
As to what to say
About not being the boss
Of my poop and it's play

So just read to the end
And I promise
Your doubts I will mend
My name, is Thomas.

Free Form

Three one day, none the next
Warning: Pooping Times May Vary
With Additional Increases, Including But
Not Limited To:
Have you ever pooped in a dream?
Have you ever pooped in a stream?
Have you ever wondered if you'd poop out steam?
No, not I, if that's what you're wondering.
I poop when I can and when I must
And sometimes my poop resembles a bust
of Katie Couric

Please Hold

On hold with Amazon
Are my pants on?
No! I'm on the pot
So they are most definitely not.
Well, they're on my legs
Which the question begs
Why don't they have pegs?
To hang your pants up?
Like my car has holders for my cup
Sidenote: the guy in the next stall
He's giving it his all.
The sounds coming from his ass
Speak of troubles I'd gladly pass
Anyway, I'm no longer on hold
My business conducted, while pooping, so bold.
Also, turns out that
That guy, was Pat.

Pat, Pain, No Gain

Sitting after Pat.
The seat is already warm.
There's a lingering stench, pretty norm

Can't stop thinking about the residual heat
I'd like to say it's pretty neat
I can't, it's not.

Furthermore, this was a sit-down gassing
No poop passing
Out my butt.

Firing off blanks
Probably I know just where my thanks
Go.

Supreme upper back pain
Truly breathtaking in the main
Debilitates me. I hate it.

Pootrick

So now it's happening
No not the fappening
Although Pat is next to me
When before, he was before me
I sat after him and nothing came
I sat next to him and it wasn't the same
An angry little poo
A sharp and hard Doo Doo
So yeah, I pooped today
With Pat

193

Steve McQueen

Steve McQueen
Icon of the sixties
Your name is on my shirt

I met your grandson, Steven McQueen
With all the east coast pixies.
His handshake didn't hurt.

He was nice, and used to play with vampires
Anne Rice is more my style
She writes a tragic monster tale

But hey, where is the staple of this Empire's
Usual talk about the pile
Of poop, I hear you wail.

Well, it came and went
With hardly a bother
So elsewhere was sought

For poetry to be sent
Like a wounded father
Wallowing in his lot.

I know, that was lame!
You're seeking much the same
As what you normally find
After poop leaves my behind.
Maybe tomorrow will be better
The poop warm and wetter
The wipe, near divine.
We will see, readers of mine.

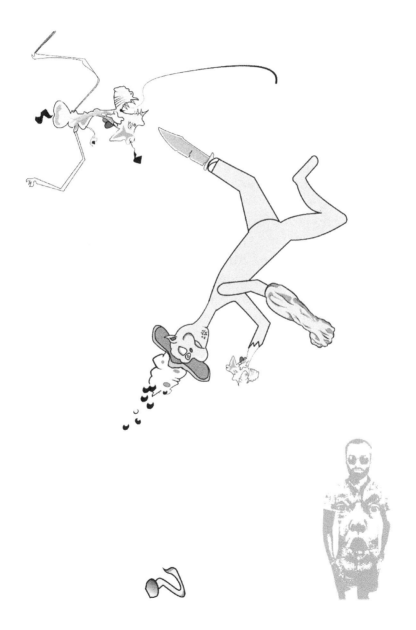

Cornhole

There's corn in my shit
On this double deuce day.
I ate that corn, yesterday.
In my first poo, not a sign of it.

Frankly, I'm not happy
I've pooped twice a day too much
I'm worried my hole will stretch and get flappy
Who am I that I fear such??

Cripes! I am frightened of piles.
Also known as hemorrhoids.
What if I took steroids
And ran for a thousand miles?

Would that make my butt huge?
And stave off that donut pillow?
Or would my ass work like a luge
for my poop to slide through though?

For Fuck's sake!
I just want to go back
To one poo to make
Each day, what a hack...

False Misgivings

Somewhat late,
I had feared
And had myself geared
Towards a poo I'd hate.

Unfounded this fear
As the poo came out nice
Carrying a hint of spice
From food made with cheer

And it should be noted
The end draws near
101 poems, ya hear!
Of poop they are coated.

And when they come out
I'm sure they'll succeed
And profits will proceed
To cause me to poop with a shout!

Two Again, Ugh

With the end in sight
My colon, I suspect, knows
And so I sit yet again and fight
To push out the second, poop foes.

I've expressed before, my displeasure
At pooping twice in one day
And I don't exactly know how to measure
The increase to what I'll pay.

But I do say this:
I'd rather poop, than piss
On my neighbor,
For the labor.

Ah!
I'm seriously worried
How can this be?
Is the first one hurried
What is wrong with me??

Two little poops
On my second poop today
It's like a giant oops
That's happening every day!

I cannot become a two poop pooper
I have to expel all in one sitting
My mind collapsing, is no trooper
I should poop only once! As is fitting.

Shit.

Insane

Did I wait to late??
This poop won't come!
Is it something I ate?
Oh no! I'm pissing out my bum.

Terrible gut, wracked nerves?
Even though it's pissing
Blockage too?! This serves
To remind me of what's missing:

My sanity.

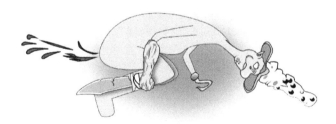

Poo 101

This is it
The final shit
I can't believe
As the poo will leave
That I will have written
101 Poo Poems of which I am smitten

And I will say don't be sad
That this volume is done
For there are more poops to be had
With more poems of fun.

It was truly a pleasure
To pen all these rhymes
With which to measure
My pooping times.

Daily I fought
To try and be clever
With words that were sought
To highlight my endeavor.

So I hope you've enjoyed
All that I've done
While pooping while employed
To make something fun.

Deuces

Made in the USA
Las Vegas, NV
03 November 2022